PRINCESSES AND HEROINES

by John Hamilton

Published by ABDO Publishing Company, 4940 Viking Drive, Suite 622, Edina, Minnesota 55435. Copyright ©2006 by Abdo Consulting Group, Inc. International copyrights reserved in all countries. No part of this book may be reproduced in any form without written permission from the publisher. ABDO & Daughters™ is a trademark and logo of ABDO Publishing Company.

Printed in the United States.

Editor: Paul Joseph
Graphic Design: John Hamilton
Cover Design: TDI
Cover Illustration: *Perilous Seas,* ©1990 Don Maitz
Interior Photos and Illustrations: p 1 *Perilous Seas,* ©1990 Don Maitz; p 4 Joan of Arc and Archangel Michael, Corbis; p 5 Joan of Arc leading charge, Corbis; p 6 Joan of Arc and King Charles VII, Corbis; p 7 Joan of Arc by Rossetti, Corbis; p 8 Milla Jovovich as Joan of Arc, Corbis; p 9 Joan of Arc riding into Orléans, Corbis; p 10 Joan of Arc riding on horse, Corbis; p 11 Joan of Arc at coronation, Corbis; p 12 (top) trial of Joan of Arc, Corbis; p 12 (bottom) Joan of Arc executed, Corbis; p 13 Joan of Arc statue, Corbis; p 14 portrait of Eleanor of Aquitaine, Getty Images; p 16 Eleanor on horseback, Mary Evans Picture Library; p 17 (top) Eleanor portrait, Mary Evans Picture Library; p 17 (bottom) Eleanor portrait, Corbis; p 18 Boudicca portrait, Mary Evans Picture Library; p 19 Boudicca, queen of the Iceni, Corbis; p 20 Boudicca encouraging warriors, Mary Evans Picture Library; p 21 Boudicca and daughters in chariot, Mary Evans Picture Library; p 22 *Morgaine at Nehmin,* ©1984 Janny Wurts; p 23 *Ice Witch's Forest,* ©1980 Janny Wurts; p 24 (top) *Morgan le Fay,* Anthony FA Sandys; p 24 (bottom) *Morgaine at Ohtij'in,* ©1981 Janny Wurts; p 25 *Mists of Caladon,* ©1993 Don Maitz; p 26 (top) Liv Tyler as Arwen, courtesy New Line Cinema; p 26 (bottom) Miranda Otto as Éowyn, courtesy New Line Cinema; p 27 *Bard III,* ©1985 Don Maitz; p 28 (top) *Red Sonja,* courtesy Marvel Comics; p 28 (bottom) *Magic Word,* ©1991 Don Maitz; p 29 *Fairy Lands Forlorn,* ©1990 Don Maitz; p 31 Liv Tyler as Arwen, courtesy New Line Cinema.

Library of Congress Cataloging-in-Publication Data

Hamilton, John, 1959–
     Princesses and heroines / John Hamilton
          p. cm. — (Fantasy & folklore)
     Includes index.
     ISBN 1-59679-339-2
     1. Women in literature—Juvenile literature. 2. Princesses in literature—Juvenile literature.
3. Heroines in literature—Juvenile literature.   I. Title

     PN56.5.W64 2006
     809'.933522—dc22

                                             2005048326

CONTENTS

JOAN OF ARC

oan of Arc was a 15th century French peasant girl. She led her nation's army in defeating English invaders during the Hundred Years' War. She was a brave warrior who went into battle alongside men, wore a suit of armor, and cut her hair short. She was deeply religious, often praying before going into battle. Her victory at the siege of Orléans roused her countrymen and set the stage for France's king to take his rightful place on the throne. Captured a year later, she was burned at the stake by the English, and became a martyr for the cause of French patriotism. Today, Joan of Arc is one of history's most beloved heroines.

Jeanne d'Arc (Joan of Arc, in English) was born the daughter of a poor plowman around 1412 in the small village of Domrémy, located in today's eastern France along the Meuse River. She was a hardworking, simple child. She couldn't read or write, but religion, which she learned from her mother, was very important to her. At age 13 she began hearing "voices" that taught her self-discipline. The voices were always accompanied by a great white light.

Facing page: Joan of Arc leads a charge into battle.
Below: The Archangel Michael appears to Joan, telling her to drive the English army from France.

In modern times, people have tried to explain these voices by saying that Joan was mentally ill. Some people with diseases such as schizophrenia or bipolar disorders hear voices in their heads, telling them to do things. But Joan strongly believed that she was hearing the voice of God. She also began hearing the voices of angels and saints. When she was 16, she said that the Archangel Michael told her to drive English invaders out of her country.

The Hundred Years' War had been raging since 1337, when England's King Edward III claimed the French throne. Invasion forces sailed across the English Channel and landed on French soil. A series of battles and campaigns was fought over a period of many decades.

By the time Joan was born, English armies controlled nearly half of France, including the capital of Paris. This was a time of great misery for the people of France. Foreign soldiers looted cities and murdered French citizens. Plagues and famine killed many people, not only in France but all over Europe. France lost almost two thirds of its population during this time. Ordinary people were desperate for someone to inspire them, and to lead them against the hated English army.

The French had a king, but just barely. The mentally ill King Charles VI had recently died, leaving behind his rightful heir, the dauphin Charles, to take the throne. (Dauphin is a French word that refers to the eldest son of the king.) Many complained that Charles was indecisive, and lacked leadership ability.

Things looked hopeless for the dauphin. English forces occupied almost the entire northern part of France. And five years after his father's death, Charles still had not been crowned king.

The city of Reims, which is where French kings were traditionally crowned, was under control of France's enemies. To gather enough support, in order to drive the English out of the country, Charles had to rightfully claim the throne, and he could only do that in Reims.

Below: France's King Charles VII meets Joan of Arc.

In the meantime, the English continued their invasion of France. The city of Orléans was a stronghold that the English needed to defeat before they could march farther south. In 1428, they began a siege, hoping to choke off supplies and force the city to surrender. If Orléans fell, so too would the rest of France.

Joan of Arc saw herself as the rescuer of her country. She was convinced that God was using her as His instrument in a holy war. In February 1429, dressed in men's clothing, she arrived at the dauphin's residence at Chinon. She had a letter

sent to the dauphin, explaining that God had promised that she would save the besieged city of Orléans.

A skeptical Charles refused to see Joan at first. He sent Church officials to quiz her. Joan was an inspiring speaker, and could skillfully debate with even the most educated people. Her interviewers were soon convinced of her claims, and sent her to see the dauphin.

Before the meeting, Charles changed clothes with one of his assistants and hid in a crowd as a kind of test for Joan. After she

Above: Joan of Arc, painted by Dante Gabriel Rossetti.

Above: Milla Jovovich stars in director Luc Besson's 1999 film *The Messenger: The Story of Joan of Arc.* *Facing page:* Joan rides triumphantly into the besieged city of Orléans in this painting by J.J. Scherrer.

entered the room, Joan immediately walked directly to Charles. She was respectful of him, but annoyed at playing games.

Joan was anxious to get to Orléans. She knew there was no time to waste. Joan eventually convinced Charles to support her, and he soon put her in command of the French army. She was only 17 years old.

Perceval de Boulainvilliers, a knight, said of Joan, "This maid has a certain elegance. … She has a pretty woman's voice, eats little, drinks very little wine. She enjoys riding a horse and takes pleasure in fine arms, greatly likes the company of noble fighting men, …readily sheds copious tears, has a cheerful face. She bears the weight and burden of armor incredibly well to such a point that she has remained fully armed during six days and nights."

Joan rode to Orléans in a suit of white enameled armor made just for her. She carried a banner of white and blue that had two angels and the word "Jesus" on it. She arrived at the city on April 29, 1429.

She forbade her soldiers from swearing, and insisted that they pray. She refused to let her army attack on Sundays. Her belief in God, and her enthusiasm for ridding the land of the English army, greatly boosted the morale of the French troops.

Joan had a very strong personality. People trusted her leadership, even if some didn't quite believe she actually talked to God. Before going into battle, she would cry out, "Follow me!" Most soldiers did indeed follow her, even into dangerous situations that war-toughened veterans would normally avoid.

With Joan leading the way, the French forced the English to pull back from Orléans on May 8, 1429. It was a great victory, and a "sign" Joan said proved that her visions from God were real.

She became extremely popular with French citizens. More and more people volunteered to help fight the English. The lifting of the siege at Orléans was a major turning point in the Hundred Years' War.

Joan next led her army to several other important victories, including the Battle of Patay on June 18, 1429. The English army was nearly destroyed, losing more than 2,200 soldiers. The French and their allies lost only about 20 warriors.

Joan always regretted the loss of life on the battlefield, no matter how necessary it seemed at the time. She wept over those killed, even the English dead.

With the path now safely cleared, the dauphin was crowned Charles VII in Reims on July 17, 1429. Joan continued fighting, hoping to drive the English completely from the land. Then disaster struck.

Facing page: Joan of Arc at the coronation of King Charles VII.
Below: A scene from the film, *The Messenger: The Story of Joan of Arc.*

Above: The trial of Joan of Arc, by Frederick Rae.
Right: In 1431, Joan was found guilty of heresy and witchcraft, and was executed by being burned at the stake.
Facing page: A statue of Joan of Arc stands in the Reims Cathedral in France.

On May 23, 1430, Joan was captured by a group of Burgundians. These were French people who were allies of the English. The Burgundians sold Joan to the English for 10,000 gold coins. The English didn't dare execute or imprison her, since she was such a popular person. First, they had to make people lose their faith in her.

The English forced Joan to stand trial at a Church court in the city of Rouen. Pro-English clergy charged Joan with heresy and witchcraft. A heretic is someone who doesn't believe in the rules or the teachings of the Church. The English wanted to prove that King Charles VII was a fool who had been tricked by a witch.

Even though the trial violated many legal laws of the time, Joan was found guilty. On May 30, 1431, she was tied to a stake and burned to death. Burning heretics was a common method of execution in the Middle Ages. People thought the flames purified the victim's soul before going to heaven.

After her death, the English army was driven almost completely out of France. Joan's life and death inspired many people. Her reputation as a heroine, a martyr, and a servant to both God and her country, grew with each passing year.

In 1455, Pope Callixtus III started a new trial for Joan. She was declared innocent of heresy and witchcraft in 1456. Finally, on May 16, 1920, the Catholic Church declared Joan of Arc a saint.

ELEANOR OF AQUITAINE

leanor of Aquitaine was one of the most powerful and interesting women of the Middle Ages. In a time when men and the Catholic Church dominated daily life, leaving little place for women, Eleanor was determined to create her own destiny. She had an independent spirit, and by shrewdly collecting political power and wealth, she became queen of both France and England.

Eleanor was born to noble parents around the year 1122, in the province of Aquitaine, in what is today southwestern France. She was raised in one of medieval Europe's most cultured places. Aquitaine was a fertile land filled with proud, independent people who valued education and the arts.

Eleanor's grandfather, Duke William IX, was an accomplished troubadour who loved to sing romantic songs. Eleanor learned to sing and dance, to play the harp, and to sew. She enjoyed hunting and hawking. She was a skilled horse rider. She could also read and write, which was rare for women in the Middle Ages. Eleanor's father, Duke William X, taught her how to run a royal household. She learned all about politics, and about people from all walks of life.

In 1137, Eleanor's father died while on a pilgrimage to Spain, leaving his daughter to inherit his lands and wealth. Even though she was still a young girl of 15, Eleanor was already beautiful, charming, and witty. That same year, in an arranged marriage, she wed Louis VII, who was soon crowned king of France. For Louis, not only did he add land to his kingdom, he gained a wife who was intelligent and passionate. He adored her, even if his subjects often criticized her for being too independent, and for being a bad influence on the king.

Facing page: A portrait of Eleanor of Aquitaine.

Right: Eleanor rides with her husband, King Louis VII, on the Second Crusade to the Middle East.

In 1145, Eleanor joined her husband on the Second Crusade to the Middle East, along with 300 female servants. She rode on a horse, dressed in armor and carried a lance. She was courageous and passionate about their mission. The expedition, however, was a disaster.

Eleanor and Louis quarreled about military goals. Eleanor wanted the army to re-capture the city of Edessa, which had fallen to Muslim forces the year before. But King Louis insisted on marching to the city of Jerusalem. Eleanor was furious, and threatened to have their marriage annulled (a kind of divorce). Louis forced his wife to ride with him. The military expedition failed, and the defeated pair returned to France, but they sailed in separate ships.

The rift between the two never healed, and in 1152 the Church annulled their marriage. Eleanor kept her vast estates. Less than a year later, she married Henry of Anjou, who became Henry II, king of England, in 1154.

Through a series of battles and political alliances, King Henry slowly expanded his empire. His relationship with his wife, however, was not very good. She disagreed with many of his decisions, and they hated sharing power with each other. Eleanor bore many children, but she refused to settle down and become a typical medieval wife. She was still in control of her lands in Aquitaine.

In 1173, she gave military support to three of her grown sons in a rebellion against Henry. The king stopped the revolt and had the 50-year-old Eleanor imprisoned for the next 15 years.

King Henry died in 1189. Eleanor helped her son, Richard I "the Lionheart," take the throne. With her son now king, Eleanor was finally released from prison.

Eleanor traveled much during her later years, crisscrossing Europe to assure loyalty among her subjects, and to maintain her armies and lands. She was a skilled politician. When her son Richard went off to fight in the Third Crusades, she ruled England in his place as regent.

Above and left: Two portraits of Eleanor of Aquitaine.

Eleanor lived long enough to survive her son Richard and see another son, John, take the throne of England. John, like his brother Richard, respected his mother's experience and took

advice from her on how to rule the kingdom.

Eventually, in 1202, Eleanor retired to a monastery at Fontevrault, in the province of Anjou, France. She went there to find peace in her last years. Eleanor lived into her eighties, which was a very long time for a person in the Middle Ages. She finally died in 1204.

bouoicca

oudicca (pronounced Boo-dikka) was a great 1st-century warrior queen from Britain who fought against Roman invaders. She was married to Prasutagus, a rich and powerful ruler of the Iceni tribe. The Iceni lived in what is now Norfolk, in the eastern part of southern England. The Iceni were a fiercely independent and warlike people. The Romans called them barbarians. They were part of a race of people called the Celts. The Celts had been in the British Isles for hundreds of years before the Roman invasion of 43 A.D.

After the Romans settled into Britain, the Iceni people kept some independence. But they still suffered from high taxes, looting, and other indignities at the hands of the Romans and their leader, Emperor Nero. The worst, however, was yet to come.

When Prasutagus died, his lands were supposed to pass on to his wife, Queen Boudicca, and their two grown daughters. But the Romans arrogantly took Boudicca's kingdom, and it officially became part of the Roman Empire.

Roman soldiers stole land and property, and many Iceni people were treated like slaves. Boudicca was flogged, and her daughters horribly abused. Boudicca vowed to seek revenge against the invaders.

Boudicca was not someone to take lightly. Her very name meant "victory." She was strong-willed, intelligent, fierce, and filled with wrath at the crimes committed by the Romans against her people.

Left: A portrait of Boudicca.
Facing page: Boudicca, queen of the Iceni.

C.H.S. del.ᵗ   Aquatinted by R.Havell

Tacitus, a Roman historian, described her: "Boudicca was tall, terrible to look on and gifted with a powerful voice. A flood of bright red hair ran down to her knees; she wore a golden necklet made up of ornate pieces, a multicoloured robe and over it a thick cloak held together by a brooch. She took up a long spear to cause dread in all who set eyes on her."

In A.D. 60 or 61, Boudicca began a revolt that sent shockwaves throughout the Roman Empire. The Iceni people

Above: Boudicca encourages her warriors to battle the Roman invaders.

rebelled, with help from neighboring tribes who were impressed with Boudicca, a warrior queen with the courage to stand up to Emperor Nero. More than 230,000 troops rallied behind her leadership.

The first attack was against Camulodunum (now called Colchester). The city contained many veteran Roman soldiers who had mistreated the local British people. The rebels completely destroyed the city. Next was the town of Verulamium (St. Albans), which the vengeful Boudicca ordered burned to the ground.

Boudicca's warriors were incredibly fierce and frightening. When the Roman Ninth Legion tried to stop the rebels' march across the land, they were almost wiped out. Soon Boudicca was at the gates of Londinium (London). The Roman army knew it couldn't defend the town, and evacuated. The Iceni people attacked, putting Londinium to the torch. By now the rebels had killed more than 70,000 of the enemy. Boudicca must have felt that she was on the verge of pushing the Romans out of Britain once and for all.

The Roman army finally made a last stand against the rebels. Thousands of reinforcements prepared a defense near Londinium. Still, they were vastly outnumbered by Boudicca's army. But the Romans had much better training and battle tactics. In a desperate day of fighting, more than 80,000 rebels were killed. The Romans lost only 400.

After the battle, the Romans hunted down and killed as many followers of Boudicca that they could find. The loss was so terrible that, in deep despair, Boudicca killed herself by drinking from a poisoned cup. It was a tragic end to a rebellion that had produced so much slaughter.

Below: A victorious Boudicca rides in a chariot with her two daughters.

Many thousands of people, on both sides, died in the rebellion. The Roman Empire was so shocked at the carnage that they began treating their conquered subjects perhaps a little better than they had treated the Iceni people. They feared more uprisings like that led by the brave warrior Queen Boudicca.

Nobody really knows where Boudicca's body was buried after her last defeat. One legend says she lies beneath platform 10 at London's King's Cross train station. In J.K. Rowling's *Harry Potter* series of books, the Hogwarts Express train, which is used by students to travel to school, is boarded at platform "nine-and-three-quarters" at King's Cross, a sly reference to the final resting place of Boudicca, the warrior queen.

Heroines of Fiction

rincesses and heroines make regular appearances in works of fantasy fiction. The genre has its share of damsels in distress, who are really nothing more than helpless females placed in the story for burly heroes to rescue. But there are also many examples of strong women who can outfight and outthink any man. Stories by modern authors such as J.K. Rowling, Andre Norton, Ursula LeGuin, and Janny Wurts serve as lessons for all readers.

Facing page: Ice Witch's Forest, by Janny Wurts.
Below: Morgaine at Nehmin, by Janny Wurts.

Morgan Le Fay plays an important part in the legends of King Arthur. In later versions of the stories, the fairy half-sister of Arthur is portrayed as a villainess. Also known as Morgana, or Morgain, she tries to destroy the king because of greed, jealousy, and revenge. She was beautiful and dangerous, an evil opposite to Merlin the Magician.

In the very first stories of King Arthur, however, Morgan was not always evil. Her character may have been descended from an ancient Celtic myth, the mother goddess Modron. In the early stories, Morgan was a powerful

shaman who took the mortally wounded Arthur to the mystical land of Avalon to be healed, until the time when he could return to save Britain once again. Morgan had great powers, both in medicine and in foretelling the future. She was also a shapeshifter, who could transform into the form of any animal. Morgan was a complex character who could be cruel, but in her heart, she always acted to protect her beloved homeland.

Top: Morgan le Fay, by Anthony FA Sandys.
Left: Morgaine at Ohtij'in, by Janny Wurts.
Facing page: Mists of Caladon, by Don Maitz.

In the fictional world of J.R.R. Tolkien's masterpiece, *The Lord of the Rings*, several strong women played important roles in the story.

Arwen is the daughter of Elrond, the leader of the elvish refuge-city of Rivendell. Arwen is betrothed to Aragorn, the human ranger who is the descendant of the ancient kings of Gondor.

Galadriel is the queen of Lorien, a tree-city of elves. She wields great power and wisdom.

Éowyn is a Lady of Rohan, the niece of King Théoden. At the Battle of the Pelennor Fields, she fought alongside Théoden and protected him from the Witch King. The demon, thinking she was an ordinary soldier, boasted that no living man could defeat him. Éowyn removed her helmet to reveal her long, blond hair, and then declared, "No living man am I! You look upon a woman." With that, she slew the villain, fulfilling the grim prophecy that the Witch King would not be slain by a man.

Above: Liv Tyler, as Arwen, from director Peter Jackson's *The Return of the King. Facing page: Bard III,* by Don Maitz. *Below:* Miranda Otto, as Éowyn, in a battle scene from *The Return of the King.*

Red Sonja, the creation of Roy Thomas and Barry Smith, was a warrior woman from the mythical land of Hyrkania. She first appeared in an issue of Marvel Comics' *Conan the Barbarian*. Red Sonja is a fierce, resourceful warrior who is very popular with readers who enjoy tales of swords and sorcery. She is often nicknamed, "She-Devil with a Sword."

In Ursula Le Guin's magical *Earthsea Trilogy*, Tenar is a young priestess who serves evil and guards the Tombs of Atuan. She meets a wizard apprentice, Sparrowhawk, who helps her realize the true meaning of life. Through her adventures, Tenar changes her ways and learns to take responsibility for her actions.

Top right: Marvel Comics' *Red Sonja.*
Right: Magic Word, by Don Maitz.
Facing page: Fairy Lands Forlorn, by Don Maitz.

Glossary

BARBARIAN

A term used in the Middle Ages for anyone who didn't belong to one of the "great" civilizations such as the Greeks or Romans, or from the Christian kingdoms such as France or Britain.

CRUSADES

A series of military expeditions launched by several European countries in the 11th, 12th, and 13th centuries. The main goal of the Crusades was to recapture territory in the Holy Land from Muslim forces, but there were also many other political and religious reasons for the wars.

DAUPHIN

A French term from the Middle Ages, which referred to the eldest son of the king of France. When a king died, the dauphin, or prince, would normally then take the throne after his coronation in Reims, France.

FOLKLORE

The unwritten traditions, legends, and customs of a culture. Folklore is usually passed down by word of mouth from generation to generation.

GENRE

A type, or kind, of a work of art. In literature, a genre is distinguished by a common subject, theme, or style. Some genres include fantasy, science fiction, and mystery.

HERESY

A belief that goes against the normal teachings of a religion.

MARTYR

A person who is killed because of their beliefs, often because of the kind of religion they believe in.

MEDIEVAL

Something from the Middle Ages.

Left: Liv Tyler, as Arwen, in Peter Jackson's *The Return of the King.*

MIDDLE AGES
In European history, a period defined by historians as roughly between 476 A.D. and 1450 A.D.

MONASTERY
A community of people, often monks and nuns, who live by the rules of religious vows. Eleanor of Aquitaine retired to live in the monastery of Fontevrault, France, in 1202. She found peace there during her final years, until she passed away.

NOBLE
Someone born into a class of people who have high social or political status. Sometimes ordinary people could be made nobles by doing something extraordinary, like fighting well on the battlefield. Usually, however, only people who are the sons or daughters of nobles got to be nobles themselves.

PEASANT
A poor farmer of low social class. In the Middle Ages, peasants seldom owned their own land, working instead on land owned by a lord or baron, who took most of the peasants' income. Joan of Arc was born to a peasant family.

PROPHECY
A prediction of what will happen in the future. People who have prophecies usually say they are guided by God in making their predictions. Joan of Arc had a prophecy that she would lead her people to expel the English army from France.

SIEGE
A military tactic where a fort, castle, or city is surrounded and its supplies cut off. If a direct assault was too difficult, it was hoped that a long siege would force the defenders to give up out of desperation. Joan of Arc saved the French city of Orléans from a long siege by the English army.

INDEX